SPACE BUSTERS
SPACE ALIENS

Steve Parker

Chrysalis Children's Books

LOOK FOR THE ALIEN

Look out for boxes like this with the alien in the corner. They contain extra information and amazing space-buster facts and figures.

Produced by
Monkey Puzzle Media Ltd,
Gissing's Farm, Fressingfield,
Suffolk IP21 5SH, UK

First published in Great Britain
in 2002 by
 Chrysalis Children's Books
64 Brewery Road,
London N7 9NT

A Belitha Book

Designer: Tessa Barwick
Editor: Sarah Doughty
Consultant: Stuart Atkinson

ISBN 1 84138 364 3 (hb)
ISBN 1 84138 768 1 (pb)

British Library Cataloguing in
Publication Data for this book is
available from the British Library.

Printed in Hong Kong
10 9 8 7 6 5 4 3 2 1 (hb)
10 9 8 7 6 5 4 3 2 1 (pb)

Acknowledgements
We wish to thank the following
individuals and organizations for
their help and assistance and for
supplying material in their
collections: Camera Press back
cover top (Lucasfilm Ltd), 5 bottom
(Lucasfilm Ltd), 6 left (Luc Hieulle),
16 top (W Drommer), 16 bottom
(Lucasfilm Ltd), 21 bottom (Jerry
Watson), 23 bottom, 27 (Tom
Keller); Corbis back cover bottom
left (Forrest J Ackerman Collection),
4 (Bettmann), 7 (Forrest J Ackerman
Collection), 13 bottom, 17
(Bettmann), 22 (George Hall),
25 left (Richard Cummins), 26
(L Clarke); Kobal Collection 18
(Peter Mayhew); MPM Images 3,
10, 11 centre, 11 bottom, 14, 28,
29; NASA 23 top; Science Photo
Library front cover (Peter Menzel),
back cover bottom right (Stuart
Painter), 3 (Peter Menzel), 5 top
(Stuart Painter), 8 left (Peter
Menzel), 9 (Magrath/Folsom),
11 top (Peter Menzel), 12 (Julian
Baum), 13 top (David A Hardy),
15 (A Gragera/Latin Stock), 19 top
(Biophoto Associates), 24 (Victor
Habbick Visions), 25 right (NASA);
Topham Picturepoint 1, 6 right, 8
right, 19 bottom, 20, 21 top, 30.

◀ Some people believe that an alien, like this model, arrived at Roswell, New Mexico, USA, in 1947.

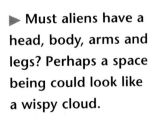

▶ Must aliens have a head, body, arms and legs? Perhaps a space being could look like a wispy cloud.

Contents

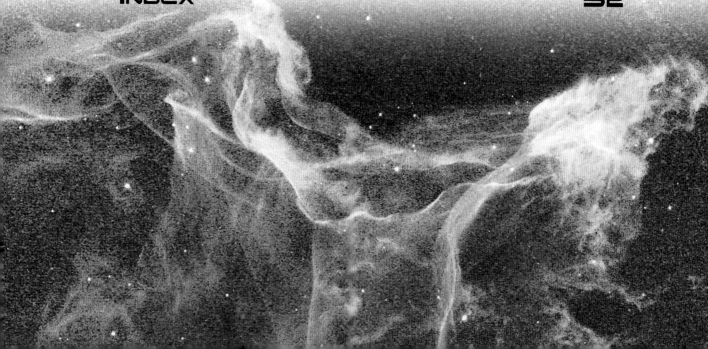

WHAT ARE ALIENS?

A space alien is someone or something that is not from planet Earth, the world we know. A space alien comes from a strange and faraway place. So does this mean space aliens exist? Millions of people say that they do because they believe they have seen them.

Some people claim to have seen aliens and their spacecraft here on Earth. Others say that aliens have spoken to them, touched them and even taken them for trips in their craft. Most scientists say that there could be aliens, far out in space. But no one can prove this. So the best answer to the question 'are there aliens?' is 'we don't know'.

◀ Aliens in films and books have bulging brains, bug eyes and clawed hands. This one, called Mutant, is from the planet Metaluma and starred in the 1955 film *This Island Earth*.

This does not stop people wondering about aliens. What would they look like, and what powers would they have? Each year many stories, comic-strips, films, cartoons and advertisements include aliens. They give us lots of ideas about what aliens might be like.

▲ Head, nose, eyes, mouth, neck – many aliens have all the body parts that we have. But they are made to look much weirder.

ARE ALIENS ALIVE?

If we found an alien from another world, how would we tell it was alive? On Earth creatures eat food. They move about and detect their surroundings using senses such as sight and hearing. They grow up and breed to make more of their kind. Would an alien do all this?

▶ Two characters from the *Star Wars* movies are C3PO and R2D2. But they are machines, like robots, rather than living things. So are they aliens?

ALIENS IN THE PAST

▼ The temple of Ankor Wat, in Cambodia, was built more than 600 years ago. It is so huge that people wondered whether aliens helped to build it.

How long have aliens been around? Do any clues exist today from ancient times? Thousands of years ago, people made pictures on rocks and in caves. Some of the pictures seem to show strange beings coming down from the sky. But they could easily be a person on a hill or a chief on a throne.

▼ This rock art made thousands of years ago by Aboriginal people in Australia could show a strange animal – or an alien!

Tales from long ago tell of powerful beings with magical powers. They could fly, throw lightning, take over people's minds and disappear. Again, these stories are exciting, but they are not really proof of aliens.

In the USA in 1938, the radio news said that aliens from Mars were invading Earth! Listeners ran into the street in panic. In fact, it was actor Orson Welles reading make-believe news. The story was *The War of the Worlds*, written in 1898 by HG Wells. The radio announcer had to tell people that it was not a real invasion. But this shows how readily people believe in aliens.

▲ Martians in stilt-legged walking machines attack Earth with heat rays in *The War of the Worlds*, written by HG Wells.

OUR FAVOURITE ALIENS

Around the year 1900, space scientist Percival Lowell believed that clever creatures lived on Mars. Through a telescope, he could see straight lines on the surface of the planet. He said these were canals built by Martians to carry water. But the 'canals' were tricks of the light. Even so, Martians have been popular aliens ever since.

WHO HAS SEEN ALIENS?

Millions of people claim to see aliens. Almost every week, there is a report about them somewhere in the world. Why does this happen? And why are the aliens seen but never found or captured?

▼ Did aliens land near Roswell, USA, in 1947? Many people said that alien bodies were discovered and then studied by scientists.

Some parts of the world have more reports of aliens than other parts. In some regions, people know about the idea of aliens, and the reports of sightings make regular news. Yet in other places, people know little about aliens and there are hardly any sightings. Does this mean that aliens choose to visit some places on Earth and not others? Or does it mean that people who read reports about aliens, are more likely to imagine seeing them?

▲ Rosalind Reynolds said that she was captured by aliens. Here she shows a picture of what they looked like.

Every few years, a film about aliens becomes popular. Soon after, more people than usual claim to see aliens. Often, the alien they see is similar to the alien in the film. Again, they may imagine that they have really seen what they saw in the film.

An alien spacecraft? No, it's a cloud in the sky over Hawaii. Clouds with this saucer-like shape form naturally near mountains.

When one person claims to see an alien, this could be a trick of the light or their imagination. But sometimes many people see the same alien, all at the same time. These mass sightings are much more difficult to explain.

ALIEN DREAMS

Sometimes a dream seems real, especially if a person is tired or under stress. Some sightings of aliens could happen when people fall asleep for a moment, then wake up. They do not realize that they have simply had a dream.

WHERE ARE ALIENS?

Humans have certain needs. These needs include water to drink, food to eat, air to breathe and heat to warm our bodies. Most of these things are made possible by light and heat from the Sun. If aliens lived in a similar way to us, they would have similar needs.

▲ The Moon has no air, no food and no surface water. So astronauts did not expect to find aliens there.

It is unlikely that aliens would float about in space, with no air, food or water. And a star like the Sun would be far too hot to live on. So aliens might live on a planet, like Earth, or on a moon that revolves around a planet.

10

LOOKING FOR MARTIANS

Of all the planets, Mars is most similar to Earth. It has air, which is made up of a mixture of gases. Several space probes have landed on Mars and sent back photographs. They include *Vikings 1* and *2* in 1976 and the Mars *Pathfinder* in 1997. They found no aliens. But humans have not given up hope of finding some sort of life on Mars.

The nearest world to us is the Moon. It has no air or water on its surface. Also, space probes (unmanned spacecraft) and astronauts have visited the Moon and have found no trace of aliens on its rocky surface.

▲ Aliens might survive under giant domes, which would protect them against dangerous rays.

Earth is one of nine planets that go around the Sun. Space probes have been to all of these planets. Several planets have poisonous gases or burning heat that would kill life instantly. Probes have sent back pictures and information from the other planets. But they have found no aliens.

If aliens do exist, they must be much farther away. It could take hundreds or even thousands of years to reach them.

▲ It would take thousands of our lifetimes to reach deep space.

▼ The planet Venus is covered by choking clouds and burning fumes. They would kill anything that lived in a similar way to us.

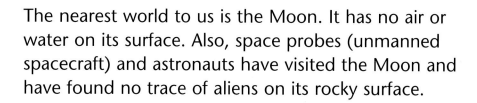

ALIEN CRAFT

When we want to travel a long way, we go by car, train, plane or ship. If aliens wanted to travel long distances they too would choose a suitable craft to travel in – a spaceship. Many people claim that they have seen alien spacecraft.

A mysterious object moving through the air is called a UFO, which stands for unidentified flying object. People have described hundreds of different UFOs. Some glow with lights, move incredibly fast, make no sound and appear or disappear suddenly. There are also many photographs of UFOs.

Usually, there is some explanation for a UFO. It might be a plane, airship or balloon. It could be a rocket or satellite (something that travels around a planet) passing low over Earth. It may be unusual weather, such as lightning or a strange-shaped cloud.

◄ In 1987 many people around Belleville, Wisconsin, USA saw various strange craft. This is a drawing of a rod-shaped one with lights.

Alien craft may appear suddenly out of a 'wormhole'. This is like an invisible tunnel through space. But no one knows if wormholes exist.

Some photographs of UFOs are tricks or fakes. They are usually made by people who try and trick others in order to become rich or famous.

SECRET SIGHTS

During the 1950s and 60s there were many UFO claims. This was a time of great rivalry between two powerful countries, the USA and the Soviet Union (Russia and its friends). Each was trying to build better planes, rockets and missiles. Many UFOs could have been secret military craft.

This photograph shows glowing UFOs over a car park in Salem, Massachusetts, USA. It was taken in 1952, a time of many UFO sightings (and alien movies).

13

WHAT ALIENS WANT

Just suppose that aliens are super-clever, with amazing and advanced spacecraft. Even so, it would take a huge effort to travel across the vastness of space. If they could do this, why would aliens take the trouble to come to a tiny, backward world like Earth?

▲ An exploding star may threaten a distant world where aliens live.

We do not know. Perhaps their homes are too crowded or they are in need of food or fuel. Perhaps their world is dying. It could have been hit by a lump of space rock, or struck by dangerous rays as a nearby star exploded. Or maybe they do not need anything from us but would like to take over our Earth?

Many times in history, people have tried to conquer other people and take over their lands. Powerful, war-like aliens might do the same with planets. We could become their slaves. On the other hand, aliens could be kind and friendly. They might see how we are damaging our own world, with wars, starvation and pollution. They could come here to help.

BREAKDOWN!

Even the best alien spaceship could break down. If this happened near the Earth, the aliens might stop here to mend their craft. But they might not like Earth at all. They could be frightened by busy, noisy, clumsy Earthlings. Maybe they would repair their craft in secret and leave as soon as possible!

▼ One day, we might dig rocks from space to use here on Earth. Aliens could come to Earth for the same reason – to use valuable resources.

THE SHAPE OF ALIENS

Imagine an alien. Does it have a head, a body, two arms and two legs? Many aliens in films and books and on television look very similar to human beings. But think of how many different living things there are on Earth. Is there any reason why aliens should be like us?

No. The general human-like shape is called 'humanoid'. We often imagine aliens to have humanoid shapes. But for life here on Earth, apart from humans, the humanoid shape is very rare. Most creatures have four legs like dogs and cats or six legs like insects.

▲ Neelix, from *Star Trek Voyager*, is very like a human. He came from the planet Talax.

▶ Jabba from *Star Wars* has a fat face like a human, but his body is like a giant slug!

There is no reason for aliens to have any legs. They could be almost any shape we can imagine. In films and on television, many aliens are shaped like people because they are human actors with costumes and make-up. This is easier than inventing a new type of creature with a very strange, unfamiliar shape.

▲ *Star Trek*'s **Mr Spock is recognized by his pointed ears. All people from his world, Vulcan, have them.**

ALIEN TALK

In stories about aliens, they usually speak our languages. But there is no reason why aliens should be able to speak like us. It happens mainly so that we can understand what the aliens say. If there really are aliens, they might communicate in a very different way, such as by flashes of light. It could be very difficult for us to understand them.

ANIMAL-LIKE ALIENS

Think of some aliens you have seen recently – on television, in films, in books and comics. Some are shaped like creatures on Earth. Birds, worms, ants, monkeys, dinosaurs – famous make-believe aliens look like all of these creatures.

Yet there is no reason why real aliens should resemble Earth animals. They might be totally different in shape, and even in size. An alien could be as big as a mountain or as small as a pea. It might be pure energy, like a wispy cloud.

◄ In *Star Wars*, Chewbacca is a type of alien called a Wookie. He, or it, is shaped like a huge gorilla.

Why do make-believe aliens often look like animals? One reason is that it helps us to recognize the aliens and understand their actions. We know something about the behaviour of monkeys. So when a monkey-shaped alien jumps up and down and screeches, we guess that it is angry or frightened. This helps us to follow the story.

SCARY ALIENS

Some make-believe aliens are shaped like bugs (like this grain weevil), slugs, spiders or snakes. On Earth, many people do not like these creatures. So they do not like the aliens to be shaped like them. It makes aliens more scary and creepy!

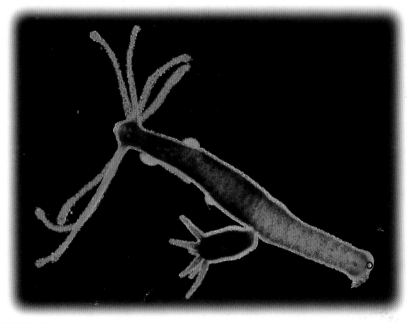

▲ A fearsome alien from planet Zog? No, a grain weevil from planet Earth! This tiny beetle would fit into this o.

◀ Worms may look creepy but they are just ordinary animals. The hydra lives in ponds.

Good or Bad Aliens

Imagine if aliens really exist. What would they be like? Would they be good or bad? Would they be friendly or fearsome? When aliens appear in movies and on television, some are nice while others are nasty or evil.

Stories that feature aliens are known as science fiction.
They can be exciting adventures, where anything can happen.
There might be amazing aliens in incredible spacecraft from faraway worlds, fighting ghosts from the past and future.
The only limit is our imagination.

▶ Ahhh! ET the alien is from the movie *ET The Extra-Terrestrial*. He, or it, is cute and kind and gentle.

Many of these aliens seem to know the difference between right and wrong. The bad aliens are often ugly and mean. In the stories, they usually come off worse. The good aliens are honest, strong and brave, and they usually win over the bad aliens. We like this because it appeals to our sense of right and wrong.

▼ Arrgh! Martians in the movie *Mars Attacks* are horrible, fierce and deadly – yet quite funny!

But there is no reason why this should be so. On a far-off planet, deep in space, aliens could behave in a totally different way. They might not even have any sense of right and wrong.

◀ In the movie *Independence Day* war-like aliens try to take over Earth and kill millions of people.

UNFEELING ALIENS

A machine has no thoughts or feelings. It cannot be happy or sad. Aliens might be the same. They could be very clever, able to build starships and cross the Universe. But their minds could be unfeeling, like computers. We would find this difficult to understand.

▲ High-flying aircraft listen for radio signals and other messages, which might come from aliens nearing Earth.

Search for Aliens

Scientists are searching for aliens all the time. They use giant telescopes to detect rays, waves and signals coming from space. If the signals go on and off in a code, they could be messages sent by aliens.

SETI is the Search for Extra-Terrestrial Intelligence (Extra-Terrestrial means 'beyond our planet'). Huge telescopes around the world receive light rays, radio waves and other waves. These have travelled billions of kilometres through space. Computers scan the signals, looking for patterns and codes that could be messages from aliens.

A FALSE ALARM

In 1967, scientists found strange bursts of radio waves from space. The waves went beep-beep-beep all the time. Some people thought aliens were trying to get in touch with us. But scientists worked out that the radio signals came from stars known as pulsars. They spin around very fast and send out pulses of radio waves.

◀ **Pulsars are small, old, heavy stars that spin very fast. Some send out many radio waves every second. Others pulse more slowly, every few seconds.**

So far, SETI has found no signals that might be sent by aliens. But we have only been looking for a few dozen years. Compared to the time that the Universe has existed, this is no time at all.

▶ **The Arecibo Telescope, in Puerto Rico, is 305m across. It picks up very faint waves from space and is used by SETI.**

ARE ALIENS OUT THERE?

▲ An imaginary alien craft approaches Earth.

Most scientists agree that alien life could exist on planets like our own. For many years, no one knew if other stars, like our Sun, have planets. But in the past few years many planets have been found, going around distant stars. This makes alien life more likely.

The fastest possible speed we know is the speed of light. But space is vast. Even at the speed of light, it takes thousands of years for radio waves to cross a tiny corner of space. So any messages we get from aliens may have been sent thousands of years ago.

Aliens could be super-clever, able to send out incredibly powerful messages and travel in starships. They might find a way to go faster than light. On the other hand, aliens could be tiny blobs of jelly, with no intelligence.

But Earth scientists have not yet found aliens. Are they really out there? The answer is still 'we don't know'.

MICRO-ALIENS?

In 1996 some scientists said that they had found aliens! A lump of rock from Mars, called a meteorite, had fallen to Earth. It has tiny sausage-like shapes in it, 100 times thinner than human hairs. Some scientists said that these were Martian microbes (tiny living things), preserved as fossils. Others said that they were natural bits of rock, not formed by living things.

▼ **Were these tiny objects once alive, on planet Mars?**

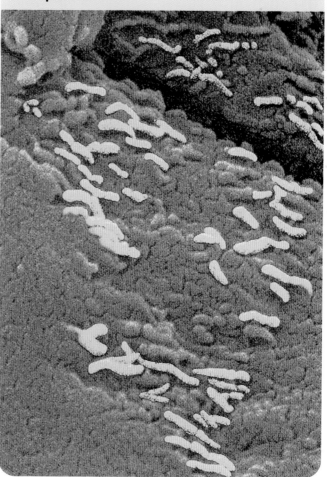

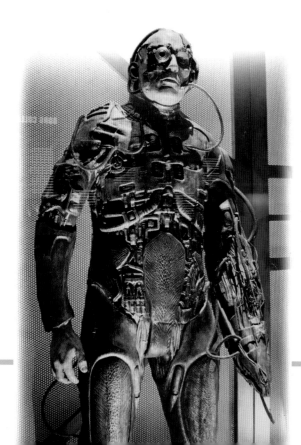

◀ In *Star Trek*, the Borg travel through space and time, taking over everything they meet.

Space-Alien Facts

Here are some interesting facts and figures about space and aliens.

No proof as yet

Every year there are hundreds of claims about seeing, hearing and contacting aliens. Even so, there is no certain, definite, complete, scientific proof that aliens exist or have visited us. No one has ever captured an alien for the world to see and study.

▲ One day, a strange craft may really land on Earth, and aliens might come out. It would be the biggest news story of all time.

Early sightings

In Ancient Rome, some 1600 years ago, writer Julius Obsequens described 'things like ships seen in the sky' and 'a round object like a globe or circular shield that took its path in the sky'. Were these early UFO sightings?

Flying saucers

In June 1947 pilot Kenneth Arnold was flying a small plane near Mount Rainier, USA. He described nine objects, each 'flat like a pie pan and so shiny it reflected the sun like a mirror', flying at incredible speed.

Strange lights

Many people reported seeing patterns of lights around Lubbock, Texas, USA in 1951. Photographs were taken and the objects were tracked by radar, but never properly explained.

On film

In 1978 UFOs were not only watched, but also photographed, taped, filmed and tracked on radar for the first time, near the South Island of New Zealand. But some scientists said they were easily explained in various ways.

Alien HQ

The most famous UFO story is from Roswell in New Mexico where a UFO is supposed to have crashed in 1947. UFO enthusiasts say that several aliens were rescued from the wreckage, and taken to a secret military base to be studied. Some people think they may still be alive today…

SETI telescopes

Scientists have searched vast regions of space, but no signals from aliens have been found. They use many telescopes including the world's largest, Arecibo, in Puerto Rico.

Aliens on the big screen

Every year there are several big films about space and aliens. You may have heard of some of them, or even seen them.

▲ Many people are afraid of the unknown. Others like to dress up and pretend! There are many clubs for fans of *Star Wars*, *Star Trek* and the Roswell aliens (above).

- The *Star Wars* series of films has hundreds of kinds of aliens.
- The *Star Trek* series of television programmes and films, and the spin-offs like *Next Generation*, *Voyager* and *Deep Space Nine* all feature aliens.
- The film *Stargate* shows how a doorway or 'portal' across space and time can lead into an alien world.
- *Independence Day* is a spectacular film where aliens try to destroy Earth's cities, but American heroes stop them.
- *ET The Extra-Terrestrial* is a film about one of the cutest aliens. It was designed with baby features such as a big head, large eyes, tubby body and waddly walk, so that everyone would love it.
- The film *Close Encounters of the Third Kind* traces how alien craft are detected, and then they land so that the aliens can meet us.

SPACE-ALIEN WORDS

alien
A space alien is someone or something that is not from our world, planet Earth.

astronaut
The American name for someone who has travelled into space.

Extra-Terrestrial
This means 'beyond our planet' – not from Earth. Also the shortened version, ET, is the popular name of a famous alien from a film, who wanted to 'go home'.

humanoid
Shaped like a human with a head, an upright body and two arms and two legs.

invasion
When one group of living things comes into or enters the place of another group, and tries to take over.

▶ **Planet Jupiter has many moons. Could one have aliens on it?**

moon
An object which goes around, or orbits, a planet. Our own planet, Earth, has one moon, which we call the Moon. Mars has two moons, and other planets have up to 15 or more.

planet
An object which goes around, or orbits, a star. Our own star, the Sun, has nine planets, making up the Solar System. Earth is the third planet from the Sun.

pulsar
An old, small, heavy, fast-spinning star, also called a neutron star. It sends out regular bursts or pulses of radio waves.

SETI
Search for Extra-Terrestrial Intelligence. This is the quest to find life forms that are quite clever and form societies or civilizations. Perhaps they even travel into space – just as humans do from here on Earth.

▲ Perhaps one of our space probes will find signs of life, or even proper alien beings, on a distant world.

sighting
When people see, or think they see, an alien or an alien spacecraft or a strange, unexplained event.

Soviet Union
A huge country in eastern Europe, which was formed in 1922 with Russia at its heart. In 1991, the Soviet Union broke up into much smaller states. Even so, Russia is still one of the world's most important nations.

space
Everywhere which is not Earth. Most of space is indeed empty space. It is dotted with tiny specks, which are stars and other objects.

spacecraft/spaceship
A craft or vehicle which can carry people into space.

space probe
A machine or device for exploring space, which does not carry people. It is controlled by information usually sent as radio signals from Earth, and it sends back signals about what it has found.

speed of light
The distance that light travels in a certain time. It is about 300 000 kilometres in one second.

star
An object in space that shines with incredibly hot, burning gases. A star gives off light, heat and many types of rays and waves.

telescope
A device that makes faraway objects look nearer and bigger, showing more of their details.

UFO
(Unidentified Flying Object) An object in the sky or the air that cannot be explained, in the normal way, as a plane, balloon, rocket, cloud, satellite or lightning.

Universe
Everything there is – all of space, stars, planets, galaxies and everything else. It includes all the things we know about, and even all the things we can only imagine.

SPACE-ALIEN PROJECTS

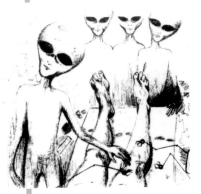

◀ This is a common type of alien picture. It was drawn by someone who claims to have been captured by aliens. Try to design something different.

DESIGN AN ALIEN

Draw some pictures of aliens and their craft. Then study them as though you were a scientist. Do they look like people or any animals on Earth? How big are they, what do they eat and how do they behave? Draw a picture of where they live too, and make up an adventure story about them.

▶ Are these aliens friends or enemies? How can you tell?

MAGIC POWERS

Famous scientist and writer Arthur C Clarke suggested that if aliens really visited Earth, they would be so clever and advanced compared to us that their powers would seem like magic. Imagine that you went back in time 150 years with a mobile phone. Could you explain how it worked to people who had never seen televisions, radios or phones of any kind?

JOIN THE SEARCH

There are thousands, if not millions, of sites on the Internet about space, aliens and SETI – the Search for Extra-Terrestrial Intelligence, faraway in the Universe. Some sites are fun, some are serious. There are several SETI organizations in addition to the SETI Institute based in California, USA. Hundreds of scientists are now working on SETI-type projects and the Internet is the place for the latest news and views.

SPACE ALIENS ON THE WEB

These are just some of the websites with information about the Universe, aliens and SETI.

SETI Institute Online

www.seti-inst.edu/Welcome.html
The home for scientific and educational projects about life in the Universe. There are huge amounts of information about the latest developments in the science of SETI, the people who are considering how life began on Earth, and whether life ever existed (or still exists) on other moons and planets.

Alien Explorer

www.alienexplorer.com
A science website for young people, using a science-fiction theme.
You can play games, create your own aliens and read stories.

Nova Online – Hunt for Alien Worlds

www.pbs.org/wgbh/nova/worlds
A large website with pages on the likelihood of alien life, where aliens might live, what they could look like, star maps and other information.

SETI@Home – The Search for Extra-Terrestrial Intelligence

http://setiathome.ssl.berkeley.edu
A scientific experiment that uses computers linked to the Internet to help in the search for extra-terrestrial intelligence.

The Planetary Society – SETI page

http://seti.planetary.org
This society helps to set up and fund projects in the search for extra-terrestrial signals from other civilizations in the Universe. Most projects scan the skies for radio and light signals from across the galaxy.

CSETI homepage

www.cseti.com
CSETI is the Center for the Study of Extra-Terrestrial Intelligence, founded in 1990. It is dedicated to establishing peaceful and long-term links with extra-terrestrial life forms, and to scientific research and education.

The SETI League

http://seti1.setileague.org
The SETI League, Inc. is an interactive organization with over 1000 members taking part in searches and the quest for our cosmic companions.

You can search for information about distant planets, moons, stars and galaxies by using an Internet search engine. Just type in the name of the subject you are looking for.

INDEX